Dr. Stevii Mills

CASH

IS ~~NOT~~

a Curse Word

CA$H IS

~~NOT~~ A

CURSE

WORD

Compiled by

Dr. Stevii Mills

CA$H IS ~~NOT~~ A CURSE WORD

ISBN: 978-1-7350785-2-6

LOC: 2020921394

FIRST PRINT USA

Table of Contents

Dr. Marguritte S. Johnson
MSJ-PRO Services

Toniekia Poole
Impact Dynamics, LLC

Dr. Stevii Aisha Mills
A Letter to My Sisters

Dear Christian Woman,

How are you?

I wanted to begin this book by writing to you and telling you that cash is **NOT** a curse word! Cash is a tool you can use to create the life you absolutely *LOVE!* When you create cash using your gifts, skills, talents, and abilities, I call that **"It Factor Income."** You can live out your God-given gifts—and there is nothing better than that!

Let me tell you how I began my journey to tapping into my It Factor Income.

The date was October 21, 2009—the day I donated my job back to the economy (the first time), after spending a year in Corporate America. I thought that position was the epitome of success. I went from Kindergarten to Graduate School, with the next logical step being getting a job (or so I thought). I thought I had arrived! I had what I call **"The 3 Bs"**: Big Girl paychecks, business cards, and benefits. However, the job I obtained was not at all what I expected it to be. I was miserable. In fact, I felt like a caged bird. I actually became ill! I had to have three colonoscopies in 30 days — two of them within 24 hours. I went from a size 14 to a size zero. I also got Shingles. It was all attributed to **STRESS!**

At that moment, I decided there had to be easier ways to make money that would do two things:

1. Offer me more freedom, and
2. Remove the stress.

I have now had 11 years of research that have allowed me to learn how to create cash for myself and teach others how to simplify and demystify creating cash for themselves.

One of my favorite things to do is help my clients learn how to continually create $1,000 or more in 30 days or less. $1,000 is easy to create once you have the right invitation and place it in front of the right people.

Let's do some math:

- The **GOAL** is $1,000.

- The **FREQUENCY** depends on *YOU*!

- The same energy is used to create $1,000 in a day, week, or month!

- 1 person investing $1,000 = $1,000

- 2 people investing $500 = $1,000

- 10 people investing $100 = $1,000

- 25 people investing $50 = $1,000

In order to be successful, you must have the right invitation. You have the power to decide what you ask people to invest in, so make it something you want to offer long-term. In this season, I think it's best to have one invitation you absolutely **LOVE**, instead of several that you just "like."

If you honed your whole business down to one thing, what would it be?

You must also have the right people. You have the power to decide who you want to serve. The right people for your invitation are those who say "yes" to you. Whether it is a free or paid offer, it has value. If it is free, people say "yes" with their time. If it is paid, people say "yes" with their money.

Visibility + Credibility = Cash™

If you honed your whole business down to one group, who would they be?

When you answer those questions, you will gain incredible insight into what you truly want to do and who you truly want to do it for. When you make your business a part of the totality of your life, it will not feel straining or stressful. Instead, it will be something you are elated to do.

I love doing what I love and loving what I do. I wholeheartedly feel and believe I am in my Custom-Designed Assignment and am doing it for my Custom-

Designed Assigned. That keeps me going, especially on those days when sales are not being generated as quickly as I'd like. Why? Because I understand I would still do it, whether or not I get paid for doing so. I do, however, thank God I get paid for it.

I am super excited to offer you a gift as a thank you for investing in yourself through me and getting this book. You will be able to get on the phone with me to talk about how I can best help you get to your first $1,000, or if you have made your first $1,000, I want to help you rinse and repeat the process. The link to schedule the call is: https://bit.ly/speaktodrstevii

This book is not one you should just put on your shelf, as it is one that is designed for you to use as a guide while you create your cash. Cash is definitely not a curse word. It is a transformative word that we must grow to appreciate and be grateful to have as a tool that can impact our lives and others' lives. I am so grateful for the women who have supported us by sponsoring this book.

Remember this: Information without implementation is just conversation. So, let's not only have a conversation about cash, let's implement!

Love Always,

Dr. Stevii

B. Wright-Jones
Keep Looking Up with B. Wright-Jones, LLC
www.bwrightjones.com

It's time to do a brain dump. Let me start by asking these two questions:

1. What are you good at doing?

2. What are you passionate about?

The following exercise will cause you to think about everything you have done in your life. I would suggest that you make a list with two separate columns. Label one side "Skillful" and the opposite side "Not Good At."

NOTE: It's always a great idea to be honest about your strengths and weaknesses so that you can always serve well, while also creating a path that you can ultimately monetize.

First, on your "Skillful" side, list the skills and talents you are passionate about. Then, underneath those items, list everything you are good at doing. From there, begin to create ways in which you can monetize those skills and provide a service to others.

Following are some examples of how I started many years ago with creating services that I could monetize.

I am an excellent cook and love to make people happy with my food. That was the very first skill I used to make money. I started selling dinners from my kitchen, and, from that, I created an event-planning and catering business that did very well for several years.

Secondly, I have always been creative, so I started creating gift baskets for all occasions. The thing that set me apart from everyone else who was doing the same thing was my unique style and creativity. My customers were amazed and highly satisfied, which brought me other customers who were also pleased with my service and products. That venture grew into a great money-making opportunity for me. I finally realized I never really operated as a business with this skill, as it was more like a hobby that I loved doing.

I have always been passionate about helping others rise higher and helping them see the absolute best within themselves. I am also the type of person who encourages others and knew that was something I wanted to do for the rest of my life. I now have my own limited-liability company where I'm doing everything I love!

I am a published author, speaker, blogger, and coach dedicated to helping women between the ages of 35 and 60 who would like to begin again. The women may have experienced divorce, a major setback, or may struggle with low self-esteem. I also help them find their voice through writing books.

I have also created other ways to make money through small investments such as Acorns Investments, which have been incredibly useful to me financially.

In closing, I would recommend that you act **NOW** on what you love doing. Know your worth and the value you are providing. Don't sell yourself short. (I struggled with that, but God has helped me realize my service is valuable, and I don't have to create my price list out of fear.) Do what you love and just be **GREAT** at it!

Dr. Norma McLauchlin
Chosen Pen Publishing
https://www.chosenpen.com

If you're a subject matter specialist or have a fascinating life experience, you could create a book. There's no need to send it off to all the significant publishing houses in New York City because you can self-publish books via Amazon's Kindle Direct Publishing system. Digital books do not have to be numerous pages long. As a matter of fact, lots of publications are as short as 6,000 words.

Publication posting is an excellent means to earn passive earnings while you sleep, and it's likewise extremely scalable. Numerous platforms make it very simple and straightforward for releasing books as well. If you have existing material written in a Word or PDF document, you might, in theory, have it released and up for sale today.

But, just like any service, there are tricks to the trade. Simply releasing publications without an exact technique or expertise of what you're doing is much from the very best strategy.

For example, let's take a look at Amazon.com. The solution enables you to generate income from e-book publishing with four essential methods:

1. Kindle sales

2. Paperback sales

3. Audiobook sales, and

4. Number of digital pages read (Amazon.com will pay you approximately half a cent for each web page read (i.e., for every 1,000 pages read, you will receive about $5.00)).

Most short books on Amazon sell for $0.99, $2.99, or $3.99, while print book publications typically cost $10.99 - $14.99.

As you can envision, the more books you compose, the more cash you are likely to make. Now, this method doesn't suggest that publishing many publications ensures you will become rich. However, it does indicate that Kindle e-book publishing is highly scalable. With the appropriate method in place, you can considerably expand your sales.

Publishing an e-book on Amazon monthly is another method to increase your monthly income. The very best part is that it continues to generate income months *and* years later!

Mary Moss
Divinely Designed, LLC
www.linktr.ee/themarymoss

Making money. Isn't that the universal goal when deciding to go into business, start a new project, or become an entrepreneur? I've been coached on how to make money in as many different ways as I've had coaches!

Honestly, the "secret ingredient" isn't really elusive. What is it, you ask?

Good Idea + Help People = Make Money

Sounds so simple, right? So, why is it such a struggle? There are several reasons, but I'll share what I stopped doing first, and then discuss a few things I started doing that made all the difference.

I stopped selling! You read that correctly! I stopped *selling* whatever product, idea, or service I was offering and stopped *telling* people how great it was! I stopped telling them what *I wanted to sell them*!

I started listening. That was the best way to determine what my potential customers needed and wanted. What were their pain points? Where did they need support in their businesses? I then developed products and services to help ease some of those pain points while meeting their needs as business owners.

The key to this successful pivot was applying the advice and training I received from my coaches: offer several tiers of products. I developed several low-cost, "high-level" classes. Then, I offered classes that delved into more detail about the subjects I introduced. Finally, I developed bundles and/or packages that included a group of products, small group coaching, or series/subscriptions. That approach allows me to introduce myself to my clients at a low-risk price. Once they determine I am a good fit for their learning style and needs, they're willing to invest more for higher-priced products or purchase additional low-cost items.

I spent time, thought, and prayer and researched insights and stats to help clarify my niche. Focusing on one demographic where I could be the most effective allowed me to develop my marketing plan, my offerings, and determine my most likely income streams.

When we attempt to be "everything for everybody, we can wear ourselves out, and our potential clients have trouble determining where our expertise lies. They perceive we're not organized and focused (because we're not)! That makes it challenging for them to trust us and easy for them to seek out someone else!

The best way to create a continual stream of income is to develop a unique product or service. I've created a service that offers clients a unique experience that helps them market themselves, spotlight their product, grow their email list, and assist them with follow-up after the fact — in ways that no one else is offering. Then, I developed a course to teach them how to provide a similar experience for their clients.

Implementing a good idea that allows us to help others in a unique way and serves them in their business is the smartest way to make money in business, over and over! In that way, the business becomes a ministry. It's a win/win because it's not about the money…but

it's not without the money, either!

DeShonda Monique Jennings

DJ It Takes A Village LLC

www.ittakesavillage2.org

One of my favorite "quick cash strategies" is a home daycare. You can get started in a few quick and easy steps!

Before I go into the steps, safety is your number one priority. **Safety, safety, safety!** That is **NOT** a typo.

Let's get started.

First, know the benefits for children:

- Kindergarten readiness

- Better communicators

- Healthier eating habits

- Regular schedules and routines

Second, set up your business by using the "Business Credibility Checklist."

Third, get certified. Visit your local zoning to notify them of your intent. Other certifications are recommended but not necessarily needed to get started. You also want to inspect your home by following the "Home Safety Checklist."

The fourth step is to develop policies. Policies should include:

- Payment agreement

- Hours of service provided

- Expectations for parents, children, and provider

- Sick policy

- An emergency plan, and

- Outdoor play

The fifth step is to find families. That could be done by word of mouth or asking those in your network, *"Who do you know that needs childcare?"* You could always pound the pavement, ask existing providers and referral agencies, and join parent groups.

The sixth step is to hire for success. Find an assistant who's a good fit, should you have an appointment or unexpected situation that causes you to be absent. In other words, have a substitute provider...*just in case*. Make sure they are well-qualified and can pass a set of background checks.

Your last step is to launch your daycare. A "launch" is nothing more than having an age-appropriate curriculum for the children in your care. If they are school age, you can follow the school schedule and just add in time for breakfast and a snack (lunch should already be added into the school schedule).

Have a diverse mixture of materials to facilitate learning. For detailed instructions or ideas, go to www.learnthroughplaying.com. Have enough materials for each child to have their own.

Follow social-distancing recommendations from your local officials. Since this is written during a pandemic, have a virtual Open House for potential families. When they decide to move forward, you can set up a time for them to come to your home to do a walkthrough.

That's pretty much "it"!

For a detailed, step-by-step guide, visit www.daycarein60days.com. I would love to have the opportunity to help get you started!

Dr. Marguritte S. Johnson
MSJ-PRO Services
www.msj-pro.com

"Know your worth. Then add tax."

~ Teri Fode ~

Wow. Where was that quote 2 ½ years ago at the launch of my new consulting business? I sincerely believed that providing 24/7 complimentary advice and guidance was expected of me as a Christian, a Pastor, an Executive Director, and a Community Leader.

Do you cringe at the very thought of charging for your services?

Formerly guilty as charged! Yep. I was sharing resources, offering strategy sessions, and getting people **RESULTS**—all for *FREE*. I was frustrated, burnt out, overwhelmed, and (your guessed right)…**BROKE!**

The day came when the words from my mentor hit me like a ton of bricks:

*"Marguritte, by **NOT** attaching a fee for your services, you are screaming to the universe that you are **WORTHLESS**! I suggest you do some soul-searching to address the root of worthlessness in your life."*

What? Worthless? *Me?* But I love myself!
I enjoy my work, and I'm commissioned
to 'give back' and 'pay it forward!

Right???

Until that moment, I had never
considered how me not charging clients
for services indicated not feeling worthy
enough to invoice people for my time
and expertise. Then, the root of reality
revealed the truths of why I had
struggled with my worth:

- Primarily, it stemmed from the
  abandonment and rejection of my
  father as a child.

- Secondly, it was attributed to the insecurities of dropping out of college to raise my two children; therefore, *NOT* finishing my degree program proved to heighten my self-disappointment.

- Thirdly, I suffered for years from the 'perfection syndrome' and fear of failure.

- Lastly, being new to the consulting industry presented a confidence barrier.

Now that I have addressed **ME**, healed from my past, and finally permitted myself to be human (accepting my flaws, errors, and mistakes as growth opportunities), it was time for me to prepare for my future!

Without a doubt, I knew God Almighty had purposed me for MSJ-PRO Services. Therefore, it was crucial for me to implement a profitable plan of action that would yield monetary results, life fulfillment, and a legacy for my children's children.

Testimony Time

Who was going to purchase a ticket to attend my first **#MAXimize Your 501c3:**

Masterclass for $197? Well, 18 Executive Directors secured a ticket, which profited $3,500+!

Furthermore, in my first full year consulting for nonprofits (part-time hours), I made approximately $50,000 doing what I'm called to do: Change Lives! At the end of the day, it was vital for me to realize and accept the following fully:

"My time is worth your dime."

~ Marguritte S. Johnson ~

Today, I am a Christian woman who no longer consults for *FREE*. I can unashamedly forward invoices and not feel guilty about deposits or having clients sign contractual agreements before proceeding with our consultant-client partnership.

MSJ-PRO Services is **<u>NOT</u>** a hobby.

I am a for-profit entity committed to obtaining **#MAXRESULTS** for our clients.

"If you don't value your time, neither will others.

Stop giving away your time and talents –

start charging for it."

~ Kim Garst ~

Toniekia Poole
Impact Dynamics, LLC

https://impactdynamicsllc.godaddysite s.com

Of all the advice I have ever been given in my entrepreneurship journey, the most valuable has been being advised to do what I love. I am a huge believer in creating multiple income streams. Almost any skill and passion can be turned into profit.

When you can focus on working within your areas of personal passion, you **WILL** find your purpose.

I am the Owner of Impact Dynamics, LLC. As a Human Resources and Business Consultant, I am fortunate to do the work I truly enjoy. With a background in Sales, Marketing, Recruiting, and Office Assisting, I generate income by helping small businesses develop strategies and plans to help them achieve various professional goals. I strive to provide value to companies by handling time-consuming administrative tasks, which frees up their time to work and focus *ON* their business instead of actually *IN* their business day to day. I solve problems by implementing systems to increase business efficiency and enhance productivity. I find the missing pieces of the puzzle behind the scenes that individual companies are actively constructing daily as they carry out their company's business and services. I help leaders with ongoing personal development during the process of supporting their business to ensure they grow beyond where they are.

As much as I love the difference I make for businesses and customers within the community, consulting is purely transactional. I have set up quick cash flows from additional sources to supplement my earnings. My favorite quick cash creation strategy has been becoming a Grub Hub Delivery Partner. I initially joined Grub Hub when the service was first launched in my area market in October of 2018. I agreed to do their marketing in exchange for some free gear needed to start up my business.

Through partnering with Grub Hub, I can interact with local businesses and the public in a customer service-based capacity while also maintaining the freedom and flexibility of planning and managing my own schedule. Their Driver App makes accepting and delivering orders so easy and puts an excellent customer service team right at your fingertips.

While I felt Grub Hub was the best fit for me due to my skills, personality, and background, in this digital age of heightened technological advances and convenience services, there are numerous companies in addition to Grub Hub that allow individuals to pick and choose when they will complete tasks or perform services in and around their communities, sometimes earning instant or weekly pay.

When considering a side hustle for generating fast cash, focus on companies that offer value through solving problems or creating solutions. Those services tend to be the most profitable and recession-proof.

Grub Hub allowed me to adequately supplement my income while saving towards and funding my travel goals. It will forever be one of my favorite income streams due to the simple structure, flexibility, customer service-oriented nature, and great pay that includes mileage and tips.

MEET THE
AUTHORS

About Mary Moss

Mary Moss is an emerging writer in the Christian non-fiction and poetry genres. She's the author of two books and co-author of an internationally best-selling book on business. Her stories are eclectic and vividly written with core Christian values at the heart of her works. She has been featured on dozens of podcasts, on-line and print magazines.

Mary's mission is to help you divinely design your words to heal the world, find your voice, tell your story and she is the creator of unique platforms for authors to share their works.

She has two books scheduled for publication in 2021.

About DeShonda Monique Jennings

 DeShonda Monique

Jennings is an author, parent advocate, and youth advocate. She is the epitome of what a strong wife, mother, daughter, grandmother and woman of faith is. She's the youngest daughter of Inell and the late Charlie Hite. She grew up in a small rural town of Kenbridge, VA. DeShonda has over 20 years' experience providing care for the youth. She is currently furthering her education in Early Childhood and Teacher Education. She is a firm believer of "It Takes a Village" when it comes to our youth. DeShonda's mission is to help 20 women start a daycare business.

About Dr. Marguritte S. Johnson

Dr. Marguritte S. Johnson is a credentialed mediator and CEO of MSJ-PRO Services, a consulting firm for nonprofit entities. She is committed to making a global impact as Executive Director of two organizations, Stand 4 Sisterhood and ProActivism Inc. Johnson is also a best-selling author, ghostwriter, and diligently served as

Executive Pastor in Dallas, TX for ten years.

She is blissfully married to Jeremiah Johnson of twenty-two years and mother to JJ Jr. and Mariah Serenity.

About B. Wright-Jones

B. Wright-Jones is the CEO of Keep Looking Up with B. Wright-Jones, LLC. She presently resides in Philadelphia, Pa. She is a published author, blogger, inspirational speaker, and on-line life coach dedicated to helping women age 35 and older to Get Unstuck and S.E.X.Y. (Self-

Confidence, Excitement, X-tra and Yes, I Can).

Bulinda is passionate about helping women to Get Unstuck from their past mistakes, guilt, and shame. She helps women to walk out their purpose unhindered from low self-esteem and the negative opinions and labels of others. She loves to share the love of God and how God sees us as being fearfully and wonderfully made.

For more information and to connect with B. Wright-Jones, please visit www.bwrightjones.com

About Toniekia Poole

Toniekia Poole, Owner of Impact Dynamics LLC, is a Business/Human Resources Consultant and Professional Model, specializing in assisting businesses and aspiring entreprenuers in attaining their goals through start up, recruiting, administrative, sales, advertising, networking, lead generation, and concise, effective, marketing strategies.

She is an experienced investor, travel and outdoor lover, and avid reader who prides herself on sharing her knowledge, skills and resources to make a dynamic impact through the lives and businesses of others.

About Dr. Norma McLauchlin

As founder and
executive director of Norma McLauchlin
Global Ministries, Chosen Pen
Publishing, Ministers' Mates Matter,
Free to Choose Ministry and the annual
Lady Lifers TM Women's Conferences,
Dr. McLauchlin inspires women to
embrace spiritual change and live more
fulfilling lives. Speaking from the heart

of her own experiences as a wife, mother, co-pastor, and administrator, she has the unique ability to connect to women from all walks of life. She has accepted the call to help women develop their self-esteem and self-worth.

THE COMPILER

About Dr. Stevii Mills

Dr. Stevii Mills. Stevii Aisha Mills. Just Stevii. No matter the moniker used to address her, she is sure to respond with respect, grace, and a smile. As one who holds a unique and valuable space in the world, she possesses a rare combination of expertise, compassion, high energy, and an integral work ethic. She loves God, business, and people and is well-known for her southern drawl, loving her parents — Fred and Karen Mills — and being a gifted communicator and connector.

Stevii is an entrepreneur's entrepreneur. With her position in the marketplace as The Visibility Coach, she has a knack for supporting women of faith and getting them seen. After many years of fervently running from her natural flair and ability to bring the "BOOM!" to the room, Stevii has realized she is the "IT-Girl" for teaching others how to be seen and heard. She advocates for eradicating "hidden figures" and highlighting one's best-kept secrets!

Academia has not eluded Stevii's path. She is a two-time graduate of North Carolina A&T, having earned a BA in Public Relations and an MS in Human Resources. Both degrees have contributed significantly to her success as The Visibility Coach. However, it is life experiences as a woman CEO that have set her apart from others in her field of expertise.

Like many others, Dr. Mills was thrust into the world of entrepreneurship due to circumstances in life. Corporate America was not suitable for a woman with her compassion for others. The atmosphere stifled her desire to be free from being boxed in while stripping her of her creativity. She found her way to the light because she needed to leave that "dark place," which is why she is so passionate about serving and supporting others.

From her corporate office in Roanoke, Virginia, Stevii serves as Founder and

CEO of Living the Life I Love, LLC, and Stevii Productions. She is not just a businesswoman, however. She is a true renaissance woman who can regularly be found creating content for the world to consume.

➤ As a podcaster, she is the voice of "The Conversation with Stevii," where she can be heard on iHeart Radio, Pandora, Apple, and Google.

➤ As an author, she is a noted Amazon Bestseller. Her first book — Cultivating Your IT Factor: 14 Must-Haves to Discover, Define, and Refine Your

Signature Brand—was published in 2015.

➢ As a social media influencer, she founded the "Get Visible Group"—a Facebook community of over 1,000 women entrepreneurs she cultivated organically. From this core group, Stevii launched "The Money Maker's Club," "The Penthouse," and "The Yacht Club." All communities are designed to support women of faith by providing resources and instruction on how to be, get, and stay visible in the marketplace.

As a woman of faith, Stevii believes in her causes and clients, entrusting all of her business moves and methods to the God she serves. She is grateful for her life, experiences, and expertise, as each is necessary to bring change to others' lives where needed.

Stevii Aisha Mills is:

➢ A woman of integrity and honor.

➢ A woman of commitment and clarity.

➢ A woman of fabulosity and fun.

➢ A voice for the people she serves.

➢ A woman of vision who sees the potential in everyone and everything.

The latter is the gift that qualifies her to help others get and remain visible.

For more titles by Stevii Mills please visit

her on Amazon.com, at:

https://www.amazon.com/Stevii-

Aisha-Mills/e/B00Y2VP2GU